START SuperNetworking!

5 Simple Steps to Creating Your Own Personal Networking Group

KEITH & TOM "BIG AL" SCHREITER

DEDICATION

This book is dedicated to entrepreneurs, small business owners, and marketers everywhere.

I travel the world 240+ days each year. Let me know if you want me to stop in your area and conduct a live Big Al training.

http://www.BigAlSeminars.com

Get 7 mini-reports of amazing, easy sentences that create new, hot prospects.

Sign up today at:

http://www.BigAlReport.com

Other great Big Al Books available at:

http://www.BigAlBooks.com

TABLE OF CONTENTS

FOREWORD

Become a connector with all the connections coming through you. That is the purpose of this book. Maybe you will be known in your community as the "Great Connector."

How? With your personal networking group.

Why become the "Great Connector" in your community?

So you can enjoy unlimited pre-sold prospects for your business. No more advertising for low-quality leads, no more cold prospecting and rejection, just pre-sold prospects coming to you and your business weekly.

How would your business look if you had a constant flow of pre-sold prospects coming to you every week? I am sure it would be impressive.

You may have used other ways to build local prospects.

For example, the BNI organization does a great job with their breakfast clubs. They are structured, there is group pressure to bring leads for members, and the members are trained on what to say to prospects.

Like every marketing method, there are pros and cons depending on your situation. Maybe the BNI yearly costs or the rigid requirements for attendance did not work for you. Maybe the local chapter didn't have the right mix of businesses that could send you leads, or maybe there wasn't a local chapter in your area.

Massive networking events and Chamber of Commerce meetups are great places to trade business cards, but it is hard to create a long-term relationship with the occasional meetup. It takes multiple, quality exposures to build trust and a relationship to the point where someone will pre-sell prospects for you. That is difficult to do in an ordinary networking event.

And you are not the star if you are only a member of a networking group.

But what would happen if you had your own personal networking group? A group with little or no cost, a group that met regularly, a group that built long-term relationships ... and you were the star?

The members would feel obligated to make sure that you would be their first priority to receive your share of pre-sold prospects. The members would appreciate that you coordinated and made their networking group possible.

And if you think big ... what if you could duplicate your networking group in other cities to expand your business? It would be a no-cost way of getting pre-sold prospects to your business. That should bring a smile to anyone's face.

That is the purpose of this book.

Instead of low-level relationships with people, now you can build long-term, bonded relationships with others who actively look for, and pre-sell, prospects for you.

No more:

* Posting business cards on bulletin boards.

* Expensive print ads and card deck advertising.

* Cold-calling prospects.

* Sending out information packets.

* Endless hours wasted on social media.

Instead of attacking cold prospects who don't want to do business with you, now you can spend your time with prospects who look forward to doing business with you.

It's a better use of your time, and a whole lot easier.

So if you have burned your personal warm market of contacts, or if you've just run out of prospects, your personal networking group is your ticket to all the prospects you will ever need.

When is a good time to start your own personal networking group?

Now.

So let's get started.

How easy is this?

You receive a telephone call from a prospect. The conversation goes something like this:

"I would like to do business with you. One of your networking club members recommended you to me, told me all about you, and yes, I would love to do business with you."

That is the final outcome of your personal networking group when you do it right.

Just think about it. One good pre-sold prospect like this is worth a hundred low-quality prospects that you have no relationship with. For many businesses, a prospect is nothing more than a phone number and a hope. Sorting through hundreds of leads takes time, and we all have time limits. Sometimes, even referrals are low-quality, and don't produce a relationship.

But when you are recommended, and pre-sold, you feel great. No more rejection, no scary prospecting, and now you are doing business with people who want to do business with you.

Now, this won't happen the very first day you establish your personal networking group. You will have to build and train the group first. But following the simple steps in this book will help you train your group to refer those pre-sold prospects your business needs every week. Once you build and train your group, you will **never** have to go out prospecting again. No more advertising. No more stress.

So don't expect to be inundated with prospects within 24 hours. A small investment in time now will be your permanent security in the future.

The big picture of how this works.

The steps to build your own personal networking group are easy to understand, and none of the steps are hard. This is what you will ultimately accomplish:

Step #1: Find a place to meet.

Restaurants are the best. Why? Members bond over food. They stay around longer while they eat and build more solid relationships. Everyone has to eat, so why not eat with people who want to help you build your business?

Step #2: Invite members.

In the beginning you will want to invite anyone and everyone to be a member. You don't have to be selective. Invite small business owners, lawyers, real estate agents, massage therapists and anyone who wants more business. Just think, "Who would want more customers?" Don't worry about members who don't contribute or help. They will sort themselves out quickly. You just want numbers in the beginning to form the base of your personal networking group. Later, your personal networking group will find all the members you need.

Step #3: Train members.

You'll have to teach the new members how to describe their businesses clearly. You can't find and pre-sell prospects for them unless you know exactly what they do, and what they do well. You will then teach members exactly what to say to their current customers to pre-sell those customers and contacts for the other members' businesses.

Step #4: Set the pace.

The easiest way to show the benefits of your networking group is for you to set the pace and recommend <u>your</u> contacts to **their** businesses. When they see how you pre-sell your contacts to do business with them, they now have the template to pre-sell their contacts for you.

Step #5: Duplicate.

As your business grows, you can decide to create a new personal networking group on a different day of the week, in the same city, or even in another city. And if your business has employees or partners, you can get them to run the additional personal networking groups.

And finally, always remember that you are **not** there to sell **your** business or service to your members. That is one-sided, and your members will resist.

Your business model is this:

Every business has customers, who are essentially people they have relationships with. Their customers buy other things, not just what that business sells. So if their customers trust them, the business can easily recommend that their customers do business with the business's trusted, non-competing business friends.

For example, let's say that Joe sells diet products. One of the members in your personal networking group has many roofing customers. He did a great job on their roofs, and they trust him.

If the roofer notices diet products at his customer's house, the roofer can say to his customer, "I see you have a lot of diet products here. I have a friend named Joe. He sells diet products that many dieters love. If you would like to try his unique diet products, I would be happy to give you his telephone number. He is a very nice guy. And if you have trouble reaching Joe, I meet him for breakfast every Wednesday. I will pass on your number to him also."

The prospect says, "Yes, I would like to talk to your friend, Joe." And then, the magic begins.

Joe has a pre-sold prospect coming to him.

So remember, every member of your personal networking group has his or her own business, career, and personal interests. You are not there to sell your products or services to them.

You are there to teach each member how to sell the products and services of the other members, and of course, that means they will be selling for your business too.

Can I do it?

Yes!

And if you are hesitant, simply think of how you are going to feel once you have accomplished the building of your personal networking group.

First of all, everyone in your group will respect you. Why? Because you made the group possible. You are the star. You are the one who helps them do more business. And this is **your** group.

Second, your members will love to cooperate with you. They see you as a business partner, someone with their best interests at heart. You are not there to collect dues and make a profit from their participation. You make the group possible for them at no cost other than their meal. You make them feel that this is **their** group also.

Third, if you are feeling shy and insecure about organizing your personal networking group, that feeling quickly goes away with activity. When you are working to help others, your shyness is forgotten. Your giving attitude will make it easy for you to be the leader.

But what about problem members? Those members who are only "takers" and refuse to create leads for other members?

Even that problem takes care of itself. Members aren't stupid. They quickly learn who the "takers" are and stop giving them leads. No leads, and the "takers" drift away, leaving you with true partners. These partners are friends, and fun to network with.

You are probably wondering how you can build a personal networking group from scratch. Where would you start? Who would you contact? And, **how** would you contact people to become members?

Don't worry. That part is easy. So let's start with the first step, setting up a place to meet for your personal networking group.

Step #1: Find a place to meet.

You will want to meet weekly at a fixed location. Why? Because you and your members want fresh, new, pre-sold prospects every week.

But where should you meet? And when? And how formal should it be?

Your personal networking group will be much different than the professional networking events and professional breakfast clubs. Many of those organizations are "three-piece-suit" organizations with officers, strict rules, dues, etc.

These organizations meet at giant networking hotel events where they pass out cards to a hundred people and never remember each other's names. Or, they are high-priced breakfast memberships that require rigid rules and quotas. Many of these clubs are full of politics, cliques, infighting, tax reports … and they have forgotten that their original purpose was to provide members with prospects to build their businesses.

Yours will be different. Your personal networking group will be based on strong personal relationships with a dozen or more entrepreneurs who understand that a single pre-sold prospect is worth much more than a list of names and phone numbers of potential prospects.

So, you can meet in much more relaxed premises, and just get down to business.

Yes, you could meet at the local gym, the basement of the local printer, or the community center. But the preferred place to meet is at a restaurant. Why?

First, your meeting room is free. The restaurant will provide you with a place to sit and eat your meal.

Second, everybody has to eat, so eating while networking means you are not stealing valuable time from a busy day.

Third, people bond over food, and that bonding provides the glue that holds your personal networking group together.

Finding the ideal restaurant.

If life was perfect, your ideal restaurant would be:

1. Equipped with a private meeting room. This is the most important element. You want to have a meal in private with your group. You don't want the distractions of other diners. And since members will be explaining their business needs to others in the group, you don't want them to be competing with other restaurant guests to be heard.

2. Looking for more business. If the restaurant is new and hungry for more business, that would be great. The restaurant would then go out of its way to make sure your experience would be awesome. Why? Because your personal networking group could recommend that restaurant to their friends and help that restaurant build a new, loyal clientele.

3. Small and personally-owned. When a restaurant owner invests money into a restaurant, he or she will be easier to negotiate with than a salaried manager from a big restaurant chain. A salaried manager may just want his life

17

to be easy, and not consider your requests. Plus, some managers find it hard to make a decision without asking the owner.

4. Close and convenient to everyone. You don't want your personal networking group members to have to drive long distances, fight traffic, and have nowhere to park. You want to make it easy for everyone.

5. Open, or agrees to be open during the hours you choose for your personal networking group. Some groups enjoy meeting for an early breakfast. I am not an early riser, so I prefer a lunch or evening meal. Some restaurants are not open for breakfast, but will make an exception for your group.

Where to find that nearly-perfect restaurant.

You probably won't feel comfortable going door-to-door, restaurant-to-restaurant saying, "I want to start a networking luncheon in your restaurant. Do you have a private meeting room? Is it okay for us to meet here on Tuesdays and give you some extra business?"

That sounds a bit cold, and there is a chance of rejection from the restaurant owner. If you are already getting rejection looking for prospects in your business, you certainly don't want to get more rejection when building your personal networking group.

To build your confidence, just go to Google, the Yellow Pages, area magazines, junk mailers, and advertising left at your door and look at how many restaurants are listed. They are all fighting for business and fighting for their economic lives. Restaurant businesses have a hard time surviving. So at least you will be talking to managers who have a problem: they need more customers for their restaurants.

Now, do a little networking.

First, go to the local Chamber of Commerce. They exist to help their members get more customers. Ask them for the names of restaurants that have private meeting or banquet rooms, restaurants that want more business, and restaurants that have friendly owners. It is a lot easier contacting the restaurant owner when you have been referred by someone they know.

Second, ask all your friends about their favorite restaurants. Ask them if they know restaurants that have good food, want more business, are centrally located, and that might even have a private room.

If you are lucky, you will be referred to a restaurant owner by someone who is a customer or a business associate. That will make the conversation a lot easier.

Remember that the location is important. If the restaurant is too far away or inconvenient, then it will be hard to get members to attend. Try to get as many advantages as you can from the beginning.

If you are flexible about the day of the week, or the time during the day you can have your group meet, you have even more negotiating power. It is a lot easier to get the restaurant owner to agree to more business during the off-peak or quieter times of his business.

Third, check out where the other networking groups are meeting. They may have already found the perfect place. Don't worry about competition. You won't have any competition. You won't be charging for dues, and you have a single focus, helping your members get more customers. Entrepreneurs, small business owners, and salespeople will love doing business with you.

Just one.

Remember, not every restaurant has to say "Yes" to your request. You only need one restaurant to say "Yes" and you have your location. So don't worry about those restaurants that aren't flexible, don't want more business, or just don't qualify. You are looking for only one restaurant.

I attended a personal networking group in Whitefish, Montana. Now, Whitefish is not a big town, only about 6,000 people live there, so there were not a lot of restaurants to choose from. However, 12 ladies met there once a week for lunch, and it was a Mexican restaurant. My favorite food.

Don't rule out buffets. Restaurants that offer all-you-can-eat buffets are great as everyone can quickly get their food. That leaves more time for networking. Also, most buffets are inexpensive.

Best days to meet?

Restaurants are busy on Fridays and weekends. Small business people are busy on Mondays. Salespeople wrap up their business on Fridays. Restaurants usually are slow on Mondays through Thursdays.

Usually mid-week is the best time to meet, but there are exceptions. I had a great personal networking group meet every Saturday morning for breakfast in Chicago. Not only did we network and exchange pre-sold leads, we also discussed a personal development book too. So think "outside the box" to allow yourself more possibilities.

Since most personal networking groups meet for only one hour, usually there is some common time that will work for both the group and the restaurant.

What to say to the owner or manager
of the restaurant.

Let's talk about the managers first. Most restaurant managers are underpaid employees, work long hours, and sometimes have little or no authority to make decisions. Yes, they are bombarded every day by salesmen and build up a tough exterior, but you are not a salesman asking them for money. You are offering them more business at no cost to them.

That will usually lead to a polite and friendly conversation.

So don't pressure the manager for an instant decision. Most managers don't have total control over everything that happens at their restaurant. They have to consider opening earlier for you if you wanted an early breakfast, or possibly adding more staff just for your one-hour personal networking group. Allow them the chance to say, "I don't know right now. Let me get back to you tomorrow. I never had a request like yours before."

Just be polite and understanding. And if your conversation is friendly, who knows? Maybe that restaurant owner can refer some small business contacts to your personal networking group in the future.

Owners? They are even nicer. Every new customer and every new meal served adds to their profits. Maybe their current business just pays their bills, so any extra new business might be almost pure profit for them.

They may be happy to have some extra business during their slower times to keep their staff happy and productive. Restaurants have to keep enough staff for their busy meal times, but then their employees sit, earning money, with nothing to do. So if you could meet an hour before, or an hour after the restaurant's peak times, the owner would be thrilled.

And what could you say? Try something like this:

"I see you have a small banquet room in the back of your restaurant. Is it busy every day? Is it busy in the mornings? Or during lunch? Would you like a group of local small-business people to eat there every week?"

The owner or manager will reply with the possibilities. For example, the owner might say,

- "You can't use the meeting room in back because we don't want to pay for the air conditioning to cool that room."

- "We don't open until 11:00am every day. We can't open earlier because we don't have a cook then. If you meet from 11:00am to 11:45am, and can be gone before the lunch crowd comes, it might work."

- "We don't have a private room for you to meet, but no one comes here for lunch after 1:00pm. Could you meet then?"

- "I don't think your idea will work. I like my business the way it is."

- "I would love for your group to come for breakfast, but to make it easy for our new cook, could we limit the menu to four choices?"

- "Wonderful idea. I would be happy to host your group. I will even give everyone free coffee with their meals."

- "I can't commit to every week. Maybe you should check out another restaurant in town."

- "Well, I don't want to make a long-term commitment since your personal networking group is new. Let's try it for six weeks and see what happens."

- "Can I be a member of your personal networking group that meets here? I am always looking to network to get more business."

Will this restaurant work for your group?

Look at the situation this way. If your personal networking group doesn't grow quickly enough, you won't need a big place to meet anyway.

And if your personal networking group grows quickly, and the restaurant changes its mind, it will be easy for you to find another restaurant for your already-established, proven group.

Just get started somewhere. You can always improve your place to meet.

Start small.

In the beginning, you might not even need a private area. If your start-up group is small, you could just meet at a table for six people in the corner of a restaurant.

Then, let your restaurant help you promote also. Leave flyers or a sign by the cash register advertising your personal networking group. The restaurant wants more business and should be happy to help you promote.

Step #2: Invite members.

Let's learn exactly what to say and what to do to get our first members.

It would be easy for the president of the local Chamber of Commerce to put together a successful personal networking group. He would have lots of contacts and years of relationships. All he would have to do is pick up the telephone and invite a dozen or two of his good buddies. We probably are not that person.

And we probably don't want to be that person. Why? Because then your personal networking group would be like the Chamber of Commerce, with people trading business cards, and going home with no new business.

We are looking for fewer members, but to have a deep relationship with those members, and to train those members to **pre-sell** prospects for the other members. That's a big difference.

You want to invite salespeople, entrepreneurs, and small business owners **in person** if you can. Why?

This is your personal networking group. You want to build relationships with these people. And meeting in person gives you a chance to "size them up" to see if you want them as a lifelong friend and partner.

Sure, you can cold-call your Google search results for businesses, business directories, the Yellow Pages, small businesses starting with letter "A" and work your way through the list. But think about it from the perspective of the person receiving your call. This person doesn't know you and you sound like every other salesman that called earlier in the day. Most times you won't even get a conversation, as the business owner has trained himself to cut off communication quickly with callers to save his valuable time.

And, we don't want rejection anyway, so cold-calling businesses from Google, business directories and the Yellow Pages might be a last resort.

How can you meet prospective members over coffee to tell your story about your personal networking group?

First, start with the hungry potential members. Yes, certain business people are desperate to get prospects and will jump at the opportunity to get more business by joining your personal networking group.

You want to start with the easy prospects to begin filling your group quickly. Later, you can go for the tougher prospects.

Who are these easy people who actively want more business? Let me give you some examples.

#1. Insurance agents. They are always desperate for more prospects. Why? Prospects avoid them like the plague. Prospects never want to talk about insurance.

Now, in your personal networking group, you can have only one person representing a category of business. You don't want two life insurance agents in your group, fighting for the same business. This works in your favor as the first life insurance agent to volunteer gets the exclusive for your group. Usually life insurance agents quickly agree because they want leads from the group, and love the exclusivity.

But, you can have a different insurance agent that represents home, auto, and business liability insurance. So your first two members are quick and easy.

#2. Chiropractors. They are the most entrepreneurial of all the medical professions. They believe in marketing. And their cost of goods, their raw cost to service a new client is minimal, so extra clients represent a huge profit to their office.

#3. Accountants. Accountants are terrible marketers and salespeople. But they all want more personal tax return clients and those referrals are easy to get at your personal networking group. Plus, they may end up doing the small business taxes for some people in your group. The accountant you accept into your group might even thank you for inviting him.

#4. Salesmen. All salesmen love leads. They hate prospecting and cold calls. Window salesmen, insulation salesmen, printing salesmen, auto salesmen, even shoe salesmen. Salesmen understand marketing and getting prospects. They are easy to talk to.

#5. Members of your local Chamber of Commerce. It's easy to get their names and to stop by and talk to them. They already pay dues to the local Chamber of Commerce, meet monthly to network, are pre-trained on the benefits of networking, but will need your coaching after they join your group to learn how to do a better job of pre-selling their contacts for other members. Just make sure your personal networking group doesn't meet on their monthly date as it could affect your attendance.

#6. Business cards pinned to bulletin boards. Think about it. These people are small business people, mechanics, florists, specialty salespeople who don't have a big advertising budget. Their entire budget is the cost of pinning their business cards anywhere they can. They are entrepreneurs trying to get more customers. You will have a lot in common with these people, and conversations with them will be easy. Plus, when you mention your personal networking group is free and all they have to do is buy their own meal, they are excited.

You will see these bulletin boards in community centers, grocery stores, bowling alleys and other places. I have even seen restaurants with their tables covered in glass, and underneath the glass are the business cards of their customers. You could read the business cards while you waited for your meal. And yes, some restaurants have bulletin boards also.

People who advertise or post their business card want business ... now!

#7. Fishbowls with business cards. Many restaurants and other small businesses ask people to drop their business card in a fishbowl for a free drawing. Simply ask the person in charge, "What do you do with the business cards after the free drawing?" Most businesses throw them away. You might ask to use those cards first before they are discarded.

#8. Massage therapists. Nice, friendly people who abhor marketing and sales. They understand and believe in referrals. And for them, the empty time when they are not booked is lost income. They have to eat also, so why not eat with people who might send them some pre-sold business?

#9. Those professions that no one really understands. Here's an example: interior designers. What they do is hard to explain. Nobody knows how much they should pay an interior designer. Architects, meditation specialists, personal development workshop trainers, videographers, caterers, limo services, wedding planners, virtual assistants, photographers and other professions such as these find it hard to advertise and educate the public about what they do. They welcome the chance to have members in your personal networking group do the explaining and prospecting for them.

#10. Realtors. Getting a realtor for your group is easy. Remember, that realtor will be the only realtor in your group. Just one commission from one referral pays for the realtor's meal for five or ten years. If you can't get a realtor, you are definitely doing something wrong.

#11. Heating and air conditioning repair people. Usually they advertise in the Yellow Pages and wait for the telephone to ring. They welcome a chance to get more business during their quiet times. Don't limit your thinking to just heating and air conditioning. There are many other trades such as roofers, plumbers, pest control specialists, painters, carpet salesmen, carpet cleaners, remodeling contractors, and landscapers who would like more business.

#12. Printers. They originally see the group as their prospects, selling them business cards and forms. But once you get a chance to tell your story, they see the power of networking. They understand that each member has a group of trusted customers, and that their printing services will be recommended to those customers.

#13. The community newspaper. Their advertising sales rep has to make cold calls to sell advertising. Your personal networking group could help the sales rep by finding new businesses to talk to. As a side benefit, the community newspaper can write up a story about your personal networking group, and even announce when you are meeting on a regular basis.

I had a great relationship with our neighborhood newspaper and their sales rep. I helped promote the newspaper, and every time the sales rep had a prospect who wouldn't buy advertising because of money problems, he would refer that customer to me. How easy was that?

#14. Advertising mailers. Sometimes they look like postcards or giant stacks of coupons. Businesses pay big money to be in these mailings, so you know they definitely want more customers now.

#15. Barter club owners. Almost every business can expand their business with barter. It is inexpensive marketing for the business.

#16. Even though you should have plenty of ideas by now, think about mobile phone salespeople, lawyers, car salesmen, bankers, auto window repairmen, window tinters, the local gym or health club, veterinarians, funeral directors, local shop owners, beauticians, personal fitness instructors, moving companies, copy machine salesmen and more.

Other small businesses will hear about your personal networking group. It is hard to keep a good thing secret. And people at the restaurant will notice you also. That means more potential members.

You can also use your present network to refer people to you. Keith, the co-author of this book, is an active participant in a running club. With just a short explanation, Keith can get the running club members to tell their business friends about the personal networking group. Keith is also active with his daughter's private school and helps with fundraising. That's another source of people who would be happy to recommend their business friends.

It gets easier. Once you have established and trained a few members in your personal networking group, they will get other members for you. Many members bring a friend as a guest to the group. If you do this well, soon you will have a waiting list of members for the different professions. That is when you can easily open your second personal networking group.

Think outside the box.

Let me list some past members with professions that we wouldn't normally think about.

- Dog walker

- House sitter

- Picture framer

- Professional shopper

- Office organizer

- Gumball machine route owner

- Professional clown

- Proofreader

- Portrait artist

- Auto body repair shop

- Chimney cleaner

- Bicycle courier service

- Wedding planner

- Food caterer

The list goes on and on. So many prospects for your personal networking group, but so little time.

Will every small business owner say "Yes" immediately?

No.

Many are unsure of you, unsure of themselves, afraid to try new marketing ideas ... and some, well, are unlikely to be successful because of their closed minds.

Other businesses might have tried joining a networking group and it didn't work out for them.

But you don't need every small business, just one business in each category so your members are not competing with each other for the same business.

So what do these "No" answers sound like from small business people and entrepreneurs you contact? They sound like this:

- "Interesting concept. Let me know how it works out."

- "I have too many customers already. Too busy to take on more customers." (Yes, and they will lie about other things too.)

- "There must be some sort of 'catch' or gimmick. I know I would eventually have to pay something."

- "These sort of things don't work. I had a friend who had a cousin who met a clerk who said these things don't work."

- "I don't want to meet for lunch. I am on a diet."

- "Mornings are too early for me ... and lunch is too late."

And "No" ... means "No," so don't try to sell or push a person to join your personal networking group. They wouldn't be productive even if they joined. You want volunteers. You want people who are excited to join and participate.

Why do people join your personal networking group?

1. Because they know you. Depending on how well you bond during your initial visit with them, you might need to have one or two more visits before that potential member feels confident that he really knows you. And there's nothing wrong with that.

2. Because they like you. People love to do business with people they like. Ask yourself, "How likable am I?" Hopefully, the answer is "very likable." If not, time to work on that smile.

3. Because they trust you. No trust equals skepticism. If your potential member is skeptical of you or your intentions, this potential member will never recommend you and your products and services to his trusted customers. If you are having trouble building trust, read *How To Get Instant Trust, Belief, Influence And Rapport! 13 Ways To Create Open Minds By Talking To The Subconscious Mind* to sharpen your skills.

4. And finally, because they want more customers. Why is this last? Because everyone wants more customers, but the first three elements (know, like, trust) have to be in place before they will agree to be a member of your personal networking group.

The hardest part is getting started with the first few members.

Once you have eight or ten enthusiastic members, the personal networking group will naturally expand. Remember, it is all about the benefits to the members. No dues, no ultra-restrictive rules.

The best part is that they are not trading low-quality leads. Instead, they are sending trusted customers, pre-sold, to another member. The selling has already been done. That is powerful. You don't get that from a Chamber of Commerce mixer where people simply trade business cards.

And don't think small. Why not have the sales rep for the local Chamber of Commerce be a member of your personal networking group also?

Remember, only one business per category.

The good news is that you can have only one plumber in your group. That means exclusivity for the plumber, and that makes it easier for your plumber to say "Yes" to your invitation. The plumber will get all the plumbing business that is referred in the group.

The bad news is that you can have only one plumber in your group. So if you have a second plumber who wants to join, you have to say:

"Sorry. We can only have one plumber in the group. If our current plumber drops out of our group, I will let you know. I will put you on a waiting list."

But there is more good news. If your waiting list has lots of different professions waiting, you can start a second personal networking group and have plenty of ready-to-join members.

More than one personal networking group?

Sure. There is nothing wrong with having several personal networking groups that send you pre-sold prospects every week. However, if your personal networking groups are good, you won't be able to keep up with all those pre-sold prospects from two or three groups. You will have to expand your business.

Keith and I have a friend, Gail Stolzenburg. He is a master networker and organizes networking groups all over Houston, Texas. His life is networking and he effortlessly organizes networking groups and events every week. I don't think Gail has ever suffered from a lack of leads in the last 15 years.

You won't see Gail cold-calling prospects or advertising for more leads. He is the ultimate example of what networking groups can do for you.

What to say to build your personal networking group.

In the beginning, you might feel more comfortable with a small brochure explaining how your personal networking group works. I did not bother with a brochure. I simply told the story of what the group would mean to the potential members, and took the volunteers.

If you feel you need a brochure, make it simple. Don't use the lack of a brochure as an excuse to delay starting your personal networking group.

Here is an example of the key elements you want in your brochure:

Name: Ted's Business Networking Group

Where: Meets at Chow's Chinese Restaurant

When: Every Thursday from noon to 1:00pm

Who: Small business owners, entrepreneurs and salesmen

Purpose: To help members have pre-sold customers come to them

Cost: No dues. Simply pay for your own lunch

Interested? Call Ted at 777-777-7777

This could fit on a postcard!

But before you hide behind mailing 1,000 postcards or sending 1,000 emails, build your personal relationships with your first dozen members first. Here's where the quality of a few relationships versus a quantity of low-level relationships is so important.

Your brochure or postcard won't do all the selling for you, but it is something you can leave behind after making an initial visit with a potential member.

A postcard-sized description of your business is inexpensive to do. Just design your postcard, put four postcards on a page, and then print, using your home printer. Or have your original copied to card stock at your local printer and cut into quarters. Instant solution.

Sometimes when you are speaking with a business person, there are interruptions. Telephone calls come in, an employee has questions, or a customer comes in the door. If you have to leave, you can leave your postcard or brochure behind as a reminder, so you have something to refer to when you call again.

"Is there a website? Can you leave me a brochure?"

Usually requests like this are a way for a business person to tell you, "No, I am not interested." They don't want to hurt your feelings. Of course, there are exceptions, but look for signs that the person you are talking to is not interested.

Why?

Because you only want motivated volunteers for your group. Motivated volunteers are the only ones who will create new customers for others.

Give your mini-brochure or postcard to your members.

This is a great way for them to attract new members to your group. They know people you don't. They have relationships with other people that you don't. Allow them to help you attract quality people to your group.

What about a website?

Now we are making this far more complicated than it should be. Your goal is to end up with 12 to 20 quality people who truly want to help each other. Do you need a website for that?

You don't want anybody and everybody. You want just a few people who will give you high-quality, pre-sold prospects every week for your business. You don't want a worthless luncheon with 30 selfish people who never give out a single pre-sold lead.

But maybe you are a website guru, or have a member in your group who volunteers to put up a website. Then, why not?

Or, maybe your personal networking group will have a social media expert who will set up a Facebook page for your group.

But there really isn't a lot you can say. This is true person-to-person networking with "live" people over food.

I will give you a sample brochure with some ideas at the end of this chapter. You can modify it for your group and add your own ideas.

But first, let's get to the most important part: talking to potential members.

What to say to prospective members.

Start by getting commitments from some easy-to-get members such as the life insurance salesman or newspaper ad salesman. You don't want to say:

"I am just starting a personal networking group. Would you like to come and be my first member?"

That is not a very attractive presentation to someone you don't know. So get a few commitments first.

The basic story you can tell potential members.

"We have a free networking group that meets every Thursday for lunch at Chow's Restaurant. No membership dues, just pay for your own lunch. Each member is a business person who already has customers who trust them. We teach the members to talk to their present customers, and pre-sell their present customers on other trusted members' products and services. That way you will have pre-sold customers coming to you, eager to do business with you. But, there is only one person allowed in each business category. We don't have a carpet cleaner yet, and that is why I am talking to you. I would like to invite you to come to join the accountant, the insurance agent, and other small businesses here in the area. Would you like to be the carpet cleaner for our group?"

This is a really simple story.

The real key is that it is not the story you tell, but how the carpet cleaner feels about you. If you appear to the carpet cleaner as someone who is trustworthy and friendly, he will be open-minded to at least coming on Thursday to check it out.

What is the carpet cleaner thinking? He is thinking, "Hey, maybe I could get a couple more customers. I could definitely use more customers. I can afford lunch. I have to eat anyway. And nobody is trying to sell me something or get money from me. Might as well come check it out. I can't afford the new newspaper ad rates anyway, and I have to do something to improve my business. And I know most small businesses have carpets in their offices and in their employees' homes. Maybe I will at least make some good contacts."

Will it always be this easy? No.

People are initially skeptical, so they ask questions to help themselves feel secure. You'll hear, "What is the catch? What is in it for you? Why are you doing this for free? Nobody helps somebody else for free."

What they are saying is that they are afraid that there will be some sort of "gotcha" later. So you need to have a good, clear explanation why you are doing this. You want to practice this explanation, because if you are unsure, that will create more skepticism.

The explanation is easy. Just tell them the truth. Say:

"I am a small business person just like you. I hate cold calls and paying for expensive advertising to get new customers. So, I got a few other business people together who feel the same way. I promote their business to my current customers. They have to shop somewhere, why not with my business friends? And they promote my business to their current customers. I get new customers without the rejection and expense of advertising. I love it. My business friends love it. I thought you might want to come on Thursday and see what we do."

And that answers most of the questions.

Remember, you are not trying to get anyone and everyone to join. You can only accept one person for each business category. So it is okay to have 19 skeptics and one energetic businessman who wants to join your personal networking group.

Get your core members first.

My experience is that it is best to get four or five members first, meet with them, and show them exactly what we intend to do. You will want these four or five pre-trained members at your first meeting. This will give you confidence, and will help your first meeting start off well.

Will everyone show up?

Hey, some people don't even show up for weddings and funerals, so be realistic. Your personal networking group may not be their #1 priority next Thursday at noon. Stuff happens.

- They forget.

- They get a new customer.

- There is a problem at their business.

- They have a scheduling conflict.

- A family situation comes up.

- And maybe they just found they have an allergy to Chinese food.

So you will invite many people, and only some will come. They haven't seen the true benefits of your group yet, so they don't initially value your personal networking group. But remember, the other members don't know how many people you invited. They only know about the people who showed up.

A reminder call is polite.

As a courtesy to the busy people you talk to, make a reminder call the day before your personal networking group's meeting. You might have to do this reminder call the first few weeks until the members create a habit of attending.

In a hurry? Maybe you can set up a text group on your mobile phone and send a group text reminder every week.

This gives you a chance to estimate how many people could potentially come to your personal networking group meeting. You don't want the restaurant to set up for 40 people and only three people come. And if you find out that almost no one can make it, you can quickly extend invitations before tomorrow's meeting.

What about holidays?

Give your members a break. Don't fight against the trend of holidays. It is hard for busy entrepreneurs to attend 52 weeks in a row, so allow them some "off time" in the holiday season.

Just remember to call every member one or two days before you resume your meetings after the holidays. That will ensure better attendance when you restart.

What if your restaurant changes its commitment?

If it happens after a few weeks, the members won't even blink. They will gladly move to a new food experience. They are not in your group for the food; the food is minor. They are there to network and build their businesses. Many groups are so strong that they would gladly meet in a parking lot.

It is not the location that will make your group successful. It is the well-trained members who pre-sell customers for the other members that will make your group unique.

The big "thank you" from members.

After a few weeks, when other members start receiving new business, you will receive lots of appreciative comments. This will help you forget about the work you invested to make your personal networking group succeed.

And what about pre-sold business for you?

You started the group, and they will make sure you won't be lonely. They will put extra effort into finding new business for your products, services or opportunity.

Finally, about the sample brochure I promised …

When you approach people for your personal networking group, they will naturally want some details. Since the concept is simple, just a few answers to basic questions should suffice.

However, for some people, a written brochure makes it "official-looking," and it is something you can leave behind for the people who have to think it over. Plus, even if the prospect isn't interested, the brochure can be passed on to someone who might be interested.

Craig Tucker's brochure used a concise question-and-answer format. Prospects just want to know what is in it for them. They aren't too interested in your vision statement.

Here is the information in Craig's brochure:

****

The Main Street Breakfast Club

Q. What's a breakfast club? I've heard of lots of clubs, but this is a new one to me!

A. A breakfast club is a morning meeting for business people, held at a local restaurant.

Q. What is the purpose of a breakfast club?

A. The breakfast club brings business people together to network and to help each other generate new **pre-sold**, pre-qualified prospects. You will also pick up valuable marketing ideas and have a chance to present your business to the group.

Q. What is a pre-sold, pre-qualified referral?

A. These leads are what make the breakfast club special. Once you know, trust and appreciate other business members, you'll naturally refer business to them. You'll learn a technique that will **pre-sell** the prospect on your club member's business. Other club members will do the same for you. You will look forward to receiving **pre-sold** prospects for your business.

Q. Will every referral or lead be pre-sold?

A. That would be nice. However, there are other types of leads you will receive as a breakfast club member. They may not have their checkbook out and be ready to buy, but they will be good quality leads that can help you increase your business.

Q. I'm new in my business, and I don't know many people yet. What if I can't give any leads to anyone?

A. Don't panic. It will take a while for members of the club to get to know you and your business. You will need some time to become familiar with other club members. Over time, you will be both giving and getting new leads.

Q. What does the person running the breakfast club get out of it?

A. He gets exactly the same thing every member receives: **pre-sold, pre-qualified business**. Everyone needs new business. This is just an inexpensive and fun way to get it.

Q. What types of businesses join the club?

A. The breakfast club is not limited by the types of businesses that can join. In fact, any business that desires to network with a broad range of business categories is invited to join us. We have service businesses, product business, manufacturing and distribution businesses. The variety means more new business leads for you.

Q. Is there more than one business per category?

A. No. You are the only business of your type in the club. This gives you a big marketing advantage at our breakfast club. A business owner never has to worry about competition from a similar business. Your business category is exclusively yours.

Q. Are there guest speakers?

A. Every member of the breakfast club is a guest speaker. Each member will have the opportunity to give a short talk on his business. Occasionally, an outside speaker will talk to the business club about a topic that pertains to our businesses.

However, the focus of the breakfast club is to learn more about each member's business and how we can help them.

Q. How long is the breakfast and what's the format?

A. The breakfast club only lasts for one hour, and we meet once each week. We begin at 7:30am and end promptly at 8:30am.

The format is simple. Over the course of that one hour, you introduce yourself, eat breakfast, listen to a guest speaker, and exchange leads.

Q. How much does it cost?

A. This is my favorite question! Your only expense is the cost of your breakfast. The club has no dues and there are no club officers. This is a very inexpensive way to do business. It's cheaper than advertising, and a whole lot more fun.

You have to eat breakfast anyway, so why not build your business while enjoying breakfast with us?

Sounds like a good deal, doesn't it?

Time: 7:30am until 8:30am

Place: Main Street Cafe

Date: Every Wednesday

****

What can members expect?

If your personal networking group is diverse, you will be amazed at the type of members you will attract. Some members with popular businesses get great new customers almost every week. Other, more specialized businesses, such as office organizing and interior design, get very few pre-sold customers because not as many people use their services.

My first member in Chicago was a man named Lou. He was a salesman for Dale Carnegie Courses. Now, while everyone should learn to speak in public, become a better leader, and invest in personal development, the reality is that not many people will.

We helped each other a lot. People would need to speak in public if they became successful in the business opportunity I represented. It was easy for me to pre-sell them on the Dale Carnegie Course and visiting with Lou. I would simply say:

"I know you are scared of public speaking, but you can take a special course to overcome that fear. And when you can speak confidently, you will earn a lot more money in your business. I have a friend named Lou, pretty nice guy, we have breakfast together every week. You need to talk to him right away. Here is his number. And in case you can't reach him, I will give him your telephone number when I see him next week."

Done.

Lou would get a call and help the caller from there.

And what did Lou do for me? Every time he had someone interested in his courses, but couldn't afford the cost, he would say:

"I know you desperately want to take our courses, but can't afford it now. I understand. But I have a friend named Tom, pretty nice guy. He helps people earn money part-time, so they can afford a better life, and afford courses like ours. You need to talk to him right away. Here is his number. And in case you can't reach him, I will give him your telephone number when I see him next week."

Done.

My telephone would ring, and I would get a conversation something like this. Now, I am not very comfortable on the telephone, but this was easy.

Caller: "Hello, is this Tom?"

Me: "Yes."

Caller: "Do you have a moment?"

Me: "Yes."

Caller: "Do you know Lou?"

Me: "Yes."

Caller: "Well, Lou told me that you could help me earn money part-time. Is that true?"

Me: "Yes."

Caller: "Could we get together and talk about this?"

Me: "Yes."

Caller: "Great. So when can we get together? Could we meet Saturday morning when I don't have to go to my job?"

Me: "Yes."

Caller: "Great. How about 9:00am on Saturday at the local Denny's restaurant? Would that work for you?"

Me: "Yes."

Caller: "Great. See you there. And by the way, here is my telephone number also."

Like I said, it was easy. Pre-sold prospects, coming to me. I am sure Lou and other members received similar telephone calls also.

Car salesmen?

Yes, my second member was a car salesman for Oldsmobile. His name was Al Cash. I know "Cash" wasn't his real last name, but nobody ever asked him about it.

People who couldn't afford the down payment on a car, or couldn't afford the monthly payment, or had bad credit were all zeros for his commission check. No sale. No money.

When I met him, I simply asked, "So how much money do you earn on people who don't or can't buy from you?"

His answer, "Zero."

So for all the non-qualified people he talked to, he simply ended with this:

"I know you desperately want to purchase a nicer car, but can't afford it now. I understand. But I have a friend named Tom, pretty nice guy. He helps people earn money part-time, so they can afford higher car payments. You need to talk to him right away. Here is his number. And in case you can't reach him, I will give him your telephone number when I see him next week."

Al Cash got buying customers from me and other members of our group. It helped him to be one of the top salesmen at his low-traffic dealership.

My first group had a hypnotist, a gumball machine salesman, a barter / trade club owner, a jewelry salesman, a karate instructor, a real estate investor, a real estate agent, an attorney, an interior designer, a framer for pictures … and, well, you get the idea. We probably looked like a carnival, but almost everyone got more business. I often thought, we just need a poet to round out the group. ☺

In other groups, the synergy was more apparent. For example, in Houston, my friend Craig Tucker ran several personal networking groups.

The florist wanted the fresh flower account at the bank. But she also ended up getting business from the funeral director and lots of business on Mother's Day and special occasions.

The computer repair person always had business. Everyone knows people with computer problems, and it is easier to refer a friend rather than spending hours trying to help someone.

In Houston, Texas, summer lasts forever. Getting an air conditioning member was as simple as telephoning a business card on a bulletin board. And a roofer? The Houston sun bakes roofs, so that was an easy member to add.

It's all good.

Your members want more business. Your group can provide that for almost everyone.

Some members don't care as much about the new business. They simply enjoy meeting their friends once a week and giving them pre-sold customers. One banker just gave, and gave even more pre-sold leads, and I never was sure how he benefited. Certainly he got a few accounts at his bank, but I never heard of any major referrals he received. But he lived for that once-a-week break from his office. People always surprise me.

Most members that "get it" practically become partners with you. They see your personal networking group as their group. They feel lucky that they met you, and many times have more enthusiasm for the group than you do!

Why?

In addition to the new business they get, the group becomes part of their social life and support group. It gets lonely out there as a one-man business. These people become your best source of quality new members.

Step #3: Train members.

You'll have to train the new members on how to describe their businesses clearly. You can't find and pre-sell prospects for them unless you know exactly what they do, and what they do well.

You will then teach your personal networking group members:

1. How to describe their business to the other members. This has to be clear, understandable, and point out a great benefit. You want the other members to feel comfortable when they explain and promote their fellow members' businesses.

2. Exactly what to say to their current customers and contacts to pre-sell their current customers and contacts for the other members' businesses.

Your members have skills in their professions.

Your members are terrific plumbers, great financial advisors, and caring massage therapists.

*** They are **not** great marketers, copywriters, and public speakers. ***

When they explain their business to the other members in the group, it will initially be awful. This is a new skill for them to learn, and you will have to teach it.

If you don't train your members what to say, you will hear something like this:

"Uh, uh ... hi ... I am Ted Jones ... and me and my wife own Ted Jones Enterprises. Hmmm, we've been a family-owned business for 30 years and lived here in the community a long time ... and uh, ... well, we are a quality company and we put our customers first with the highest quality customer service. Most of our customers come back over and over not because we are the cheapest, but because we are the best and we care about them and they know we care about them ... uh, and we are dependable. Thank you."

The other members don't even know what Ted does! Is he a dentist, a circus performer? Does he sell lighting to businesses?

And why should the other members be excited about his business? Why should the other businesses recommend Ted's business to their current customers?

This is not Ted's fault though. It is our fault for not coaching Ted on exactly what to say during his 30-second business introduction to the group. Ted did not study or learn marketing or public speaking. Ted learned the skills of his business instead.

So let's help Ted and all of our members do a great job of explaining exactly what they do, and maybe even help them tell us what to say to our customers so our customers would like to do business with Ted.

The 30-second commercial.

During your personal networking group meeting, each member has the opportunity to give a little commercial about what he does. You go around the table and, one by one, your members **stand up** and say:

- Their name and the name of their business.

- Where their business is located.

- Exactly what they do.

- Why our contacts would love doing business with them.

- Who would be their ideal customer.

Now, with only 30 seconds to say all that ... we had better help them be efficient. We have to help them organize and say things clearly and concisely.

Why is this important? Because the members can't remember a two-minute presentation by everyone. Mind overload! However, the members could remember one great sentence about what a member does, and one great sentence about why to do business with that member.

Another reason to keep it to 30 seconds? How about this?

For someone who is scared to stand up and speak, 30 seconds is manageable, not too intimidating. Asking someone to speak to a group can cause some small business people to have a panic attack. But 30 seconds? That can be taught and memorized quickly.

Need yet another reason? If you don't limit it to 30 seconds, you will have some members that will talk and talk and talk and talk ... and the other members will resent that.

Suggestion: Before a new member's first personal networking group meeting, sit down with him and help the new member with his 30-second speech. Your new member will appreciate it. You will appreciate it. And your group will appreciate it.

If your group has a problem keeping their 30-second commercials short, have a little light-hearted hint. Purchase a timer. And then when the speaker goes over his time, you can wave, or give a sign to wrap it up. Oh, and you don't always have to be the bad guy. You can get other members to be the timer also.

Examples of 30-second commercials.

Again, these are the five main points in the 30-second commercial:

- Their name and the name of their business.

- Where their business is located.

- Exactly what they do.

- Why our contacts would love doing business with them.

- Who would be their ideal customer.

So let's try some 30-second commercials right now.

The insurance agent.

Hi, my name is Joe Smith. I am a life insurance agent with Big Time Insurance Company, and I live right here in Hometown, Texas. Insurance is confusing because there are hundreds of policies to choose from. I sort out these insurance options for people and get them the lowest price for what they need. No more headaches or worries about being ripped off. My ideal customer is someone who just got married, or is going to have more children and knows they need insurance.

The diet products salesperson.

Hi, my name is Mary Jones. I sell the Slimmer Body Diet breakfast drink and I live right here in Hometown,

Texas. I show people how to lose weight just by changing what they have for breakfast. They just drink delicious milkshakes for breakfast. No more gym memberships or starving or counting calories. My ideal customer is someone who wants to lose weight, but is too busy to exercise and cook organic foods. Oh, and it is perfect for overweight children too.

The roofing contractor.

Hi, my name is Jerry Johnson. I repair roofs and live here in Hometown, Texas. Hail storms and wind storms ruin roofs, and some roofs just wear out. I can repair or put on a new roof and guarantee my work, and if the roof was damaged by a storm, most times the insurance company pays the whole cost. My ideal prospect is someone with an old roof who wants it replaced hassle-free.

The cosmetic salesperson.

Hi, my name is Heather Lee. I show women how to use makeup that makes them more beautiful. I live here in Hometown, Texas. All women use makeup, but they end up buying makeup that doesn't match. I can fix that. My ideal prospect is a lady who goes to work daily, wants to look good, but doesn't want to spend hours messing around with makeup.

The architect.

Hi, my name is John Wilson, and I am a private architect who lives in Next Door, Texas. Many people want a dream home that they design, not just a house that looks like all the others. I help them design it and create the plans for building their home. They need me to get their home construction approved. My ideal prospect is someone who wants a vacation house on Lake Awesome.

The travel agent.

Hi, my name is Terry Matthews, and I own Matthews Travel Agency here in Hometown, Texas. People can get their airline tickets and hotels on the Internet, but they need help in planning a vacation to other countries. I specialize in European vacations and also Caribbean cruises. My ideal prospect is a family who want to take a pre-planned vacation with no hassles.

Don't pitch the members.

As you can see, these 30-second commercials are not designed to sell the members in attendance. They are designed to:

1. Help the members in attendance understand what the person does.

2. Help the other members think of who they know that might be an ideal prospect.

3. Help the other members know what they could say to a friend or customer about that member's business.

Creating a 30-second speech might be intimidating for many new members. Help them. Once they have a basic 30-second speech, they can improve it slightly over time. Your personal networking group members will learn quickly.

Just use the previous examples as a basic template.

What if they have a technical business?

Technical businesses have their own jargon, abbreviations, and are often not understood by others. We have to translate these technical business products and services into something that the other members understand, and can pass along to their customers.

I find these two words help a lot:

"Which means …"

Here is an example. A member might say:

"Hi, my name is Nathan Nerd, and I own Nerd's IT Consultancy here in Hometown, Texas. CIOs need help implementing ERPs into their business, and I specialize in SAP installations. My ideal prospect is the CEO of a multi-million dollar company in need of an ERP solution."

What ?????? How can the insurance agent pass that along to a customer?

This 30-second commercial needs the "which means" translation.

Now, it should sound like this:

The computer nerd.

"Hi, my name is Nathan Nerd, and I own Nerd's IT Consultancy here in Hometown, Texas. Big companies have big problems coordinating accounting, inventories, and marketing. I am an IT consultant **which means** I help companies move their computers and accounting from the Stone Age into a cool system that every big business needs. My ideal prospect is a top executive at a big company, who wants the computers updated with no hassles.

Still having problems getting businesses to explain what they do clearly to other members?

Try this.

Explain to the business person the difference between **features** and **benefits**.

A **feature** is what the business does.

A **benefit** is what the business does that makes the customer happy.

You want your business people to explain the benefits in their 30-second commercial. That's what will get the potential customers excited.

Here are some examples of the difference:

Feature: I use copper pipe in all my plumbing.

Benefit: I use copper pipe because it will last almost forever, and you won't need a plumber again.

Feature: I do financial estate planning.

Benefit: I help you arrange your finances so the government takes less of your money.

Feature: We use web presses for our larger jobs.

Benefit: Our web presses can make your big jobs inexpensive so you have more money left over for your business.

Feature: I sell color-coordinated makeup.

Benefit: Our complete makeup line instantly matches so you won't look like a circus clown when you leave your home.

It gets easier with just a little practice. You will have to do the practicing though, as your members don't know what to practice.

And if it is still hard to understand what the business person does, try this.

Just fill in the blanks to the following statements:

When you use my service or product, here is what happens:

_____.

When you try my service or product, this is what you can expect:

_____.

So here are a few examples of how that would sound:

1. When you use my travel service, here is what happens. You make just one phone call to me, and I shop all the secret places to find you the best price for your travel.

2. When you use our quick-printing services, here is what happens. You drop off your printing before 5:00pm, and we do your entire print job overnight, so you can pick up your print job at 8:00am the next day.

3. When you use our diet products, here is what you can expect. Every morning you drink this breakfast shake, and you will be full until lunch with no donut cravings.

4. When you use our custom sign service, here is what you can expect. We make a custom sign that stands out, so when cars pass your sign, they think of you.

The 30-second commercial is the most important part of the personal networking group meetings. Nobody can sell the services or products of another member, unless they understand who they are and what they do.

With a great 30-second commercial, and some time to build relationships, the members of your personal networking group will gladly pre-sell you to the people they know.

Your weekly group meeting.

Why meet weekly as a group? Why not simple one-on-one meetings with your members?

Because if you want your personal networking group to prosper, they have to do business with each other, not just with you.

Chances are that you don't have enough new contacts to keep every member happy. To keep your personal networking group members involved, they need the other members to help send them pre-sold prospects and customers.

If you meet personally with a member to exchange pre-sold prospects, you are robbing that member of the chance to receive pre-sold prospects from the other members.

Your weekly group meeting builds the community and constantly reinforces to everyone that you are the glue that holds the group together.

The good news is that your members are all volunteers. They were not forced to come. They wanted to come!

These will be some of the most helpful business associates you will ever come to know. They appreciate that you make this networking group possible to relieve them of cold-calling prospects, expensive advertising, and lonely periods of no sales.

They love you.

Some general points of setup.

1. Don't set up your meeting "classroom style" with everyone facing one way. This is a networking group. You want people to talk to people, so get them seated at a round table or facing each other across a rectangular table. The real relationships are built while business people talk to each other.

2. Mingle and rotate. Don't let members sit with the same business friends each week. They already know these people. Try to set the tone every time by having members sit with different members when possible. The deeper each member understands the other members' businesses, the easier it will be to recommend and promote these businesses to their current customers and contacts.

3. You don't want members exchanging literature and business cards during your meeting. That would remind them of those "other networking events" where everyone just pushed for more business for themselves.

Do this with class. Have one place, preferably an empty table, where all the members can leave literature and business cards. If any member is interested, that member can pick up just the literature he needs.

If you don't do this, you will get pushy guests coming to your meetings pitching everyone, handing out packets of information … because the guest hasn't yet learned that it is the quality of the relationship, not the quantity of information passed out.

Also, when the members give their short 30-second commercials during the meeting, they can just refer people to the information table for more literature or business cards. If every member spoke for 30 seconds, and then spent another minute or two giving out information, your meeting would run too long.

You certainly don't want people passing out information when they should be paying attention to the next speaker.

So what format should I use for my meeting?

It will be your personal networking group and you have the freedom to adjust the format to your needs, and the group's needs.

Here is one format that you can adjust to your needs.

7:30am - 7:45am. Social time. People come late, new guests want to know what to do. Food that was ordered is arriving. Your members want to talk, things are happening, and there's no use trying to talk over the chaos.

7:45am. Take control. Start with a quick reminder that this personal networking group exists not as a social club, but as a serious way to help each other in business by pre-selling your customers on the services and products of other members.

7:46am. Welcome any new members and guests. Remind everyone that there is only one person in the group for each business category, so we all want to offer the best products and services in our category. Why is this reminder important? Sometimes a guest will attend who represents a service or product that is already represented by a current member. The guest will understand why he can't join this group, and will be more pleasant when you ask him to be on a waiting list.

7:50am. This is where business happens. Each member, one by one, **stands** and does the following:

A. Gives his 30-second presentation of what he does and the type of prospect he is looking for.

B. Acknowledges and thanks individual members who provided him with pre-sold prospects the previous week, and if appropriate, states if those pre-sold prospects became customers.

C. **Publicly** gives out pre-sold prospects to fellow members that he developed during the week. Publicly is important. It sets the standard for the others to follow to feel obligated to create pre-sold prospects also. A member would feel embarrassed to say week after week after week, "And I have no pre-sold prospects for anybody here." A little group pressure helps members remember that they not only receive, but they have to give also.

The entire process might take one minute per member. So, if you have ten members, in 10-15 minutes the most important part of the meeting is accomplished.

8:10am. This week's main speaker talks for 15 minutes. Who is the main speaker?

1. If you are lucky, maybe one of the members has a contact with special skills or information to pass on to the group. I have had hypnotists talk about confidence, newspaper editors talk about how to get free publicity, wardrobe experts, sales trainers and time management consultants. Everyone enjoys a little variety each week.

2. If you have no special speaker for the week, then one of the members gets 10 minutes to describe his business in more detail to the group. Caution: Give this member advance notice so he can prepare. Then, after your member has prepared, do a little coaching to help him make his speech even better. Remember, your members are experts in their business, not expert public speakers.

8:25am. Final words from you. Remind the members that if they want more pre-sold prospects, all they have to do is get more members. Ask them to make the effort to tell other non-competing businesses about your group.

8:30am. Finish. There is nothing worse than a meeting that runs late. Be adamant about always finishing on time. You can start late, but if you don't finish on time, your members become stressed as they have other plans for the day.

Will this format be your format?

You'll probably use something similar. You only have one hour of their time, so you will want to squeeze in these important elements.

But remember, these are **independent** business people. So don't make things too rigid with penalties and grammar school discipline. Stay focused on the ultimate goal: new business for members of your personal networking group.

Your main speaker.

You want to keep your group interested and have something to look forward to. An engaging guest speaker every week fills that need.

You can get an outside speaker with an interesting expertise for the price of breakfast. This is not a budget breaker.

Where can you find interesting speakers with knowledge your personal networking group wants? Here are some ideas.

1. Any politician. Politicians love to talk, and love making new contacts. Of course you will give the politician the topic your group wants to hear. You don't want to hear the politician's fundraising speech. And your fellow personal networking group members would love having a chance to make contact with a local politician. That could be an important contact for them later.

The politician could talk on the projects planned for the local community, where to get help for loans and government assistance, who to write in Congress and what to say.

2. A local sports hero. Just a few interesting inside stories would be fun. Your members can then always tell their friends that they had breakfast with him.

3. A local commercial banker. He or she could talk about how to get a business loan, how to prepare the

documents, the details a bank looks for, how to go to the Small Business Administration for loans, and more. Other potential topics: the differences in business banking accounts, how to get a letter of credit, financial trends, etc.

4. Toastmasters. The members love to practice, and many have interesting stories your members would enjoy.

5. A business teacher from a local college. We all need to know more about business, so why not learn while enjoying breakfast?

6. A local author. Hopefully it would be an author with a book about marketing or business. Or, how about a motivational speaker?

7. A health expert. Maybe someone who knows about herbal remedies, or a dieting expert to confirm that breakfast is the most important meal of the day. Or maybe someone certified in teaching CPR.

8. A local charity organization that will describe the work they are doing in the community.

9. A private investigator who shows how he tracks down information and who shares a few fun stories.

Try to arrange as many interesting guest speakers as you can, and then when no speaker is available, you can have someone in your personal networking group be the main speaker to fill in.

Guest speakers will help to keep your group fresh and engaged.

What your members do during the week.

Let's look at the local real estate agent. After selling a home to a new client, the real estate agent might say, "Have you met anyone yet in the community?"

The client trusts the local real estate agent. The client has spent thousands of dollars based upon the agent's recommendation.

So the client answers, "No, haven't met anyone yet. We don't know anyone yet in our new community. So do you have any recommendations for a family dentist, a new carpet installer, a doctor, a health food store and a local banker?"

Of course the agent recommends the trusted business members from your personal networking group.

What about the realtor's new client? Well, the client is very happy to be referred to positive people that can be trusted. Most people who move to new cities are looking forward to new friends, new relationships, and are tired of hanging around with whiners and negative in-laws.

This win-win situation makes the new person in town happy, and makes your fellow members of your personal networking group happy also.

What about the accountant in your personal networking group? When a client has his personal income tax reviewed, the accountant could recommend, "You might want to consider a part-time business to reduce your tax liability."

If the client feels this would be a good solution, the accountant could recommend the network marketer from your personal networking group.

What about the dentist? A mother brings three of her children for their dental checkup. The dentist could ask if they plan on a family vacation this year. That would be an easy pre-sold customer for the travel agent in your personal networking group.

Don't be pushy.

Teach your fellow members to recommend, not sell. People don't like to be sold to, but they do appreciate sincere recommendations.

For example, what if one of your customers wants to buy a Mercedes automobile, and your personal networking group member only sells Toyotas? Pushing your customer to go to a Toyota dealership to talk to your friend would be rude, a hard sell, and definitely not in your customer's best interest.

What about social contacts as pre-sold prospects for your personal networking group?

Sure, lots of businesses have an easy time referring their current customers and clients.

But let's think about personal relationships and personal contacts also. Everyone has friends, relatives, and social contacts that are met on a daily basis.

Eventually, almost everyone will need a lawyer, an accountant, a real estate agent, an insurance agent, a printer, a new car, a vacation, and even a baby-sitter or a massage.

Everyone in your personal networking group can easily pre-sell their personal contacts on the services and products of the other members.

So, the business plan is simple. Politely recommend your contacts to other members, and they do the same.

And since you are the epicenter and organizer of your personal networking group, you will be constantly rewarded with plenty of pre-sold prospects from your members who appreciate all that you do for them.

Step #4: Set the pace.

The easiest way to show the benefits of your networking group is for you to set the pace and be a great recommender of your contacts to their businesses.

When your personal networking group sees how you pre-sell your contacts to do business with them, they now have the template to pre-sell their contacts for you.

Giving and getting pre-sold prospects is the reason your personal networking group exists.

As you set the pace by giving more pre-sold leads than you receive, the members quickly catch on that they need to be more of a giver than a taker.

Look at it this way. Let's say that you are the printer in the personal networking group. Each week you receive pre-sold prospects from some of the other members, and when it is time, you give your 30-second commercial for your business, and announce, "And I don't have any pre-sold prospects for anyone here."

After a few weeks, that gets pretty embarrassing. You look like a selfish person simply taking advantage of everyone. So what would you do? Force yourself to get some pre-sold prospects for next week, of course.

And if you are generous, and consistently give more pre-sold prospects than you receive, the other members will notice. They will go out of their way to promote you even more.

Remember, it is the giving of pre-sold prospects, not the getting, that counts.

That is why the pre-sold prospects are distributed publicly at your personal networking group. Your group members will be quick to catch on.

Your 30-second commercial.

One good example you can give to your members is to keep your 30-second commercial the same week after week. Why?

Over time they will know and understand your business better, and then it is much easier for them to recommend your business when appropriate. It is almost like giving the other members a script to say when they recommend you to one of their contacts.

Remember to thank the members who gave you pre-sold prospects the week before, and if appropriate, you can tell them if their referral was successful for your business. Members loved to be thanked. The feeling of appreciation is a strong motivator to get the members to do more.

The more you do for your personal networking group, the more your personal networking group will do for you.

Different types of prospects.

When giving and receiving pre-sold prospects and leads, not every prospect is equal. Here are the three most common types of prospects and leads that will be given at your personal networking group meeting.

Type #1: The pre-sold prospect.

This is the best possible type of prospect. The prospect is qualified, is ready to buy, and has so much trust in the referrer that your sale is almost guaranteed. If life was perfect, every prospect would be this type, but as we know, life isn't perfect.

Let me give you an example of this type of prospect.

I injured my shoulder playing sports. Yes, I tore my rotator cuff and several tendons pitching wiffle ball. Embarrassing.

Two shoulder surgeries later, I still had constant pain. A friend I trusted recommended acupuncture.

My initial reaction, "Are you kidding? No way!"

But because I respected my friend, and trusted his recommendations, I walked into the recommended acupuncture office and basically said, "Here is all my money. Start needling me now."

Another example:

I had a contact who desperately needed to be able to speak publicly for her business. However, she was nervous, self-conscious, and cried just thinking about it.

I said to her, "I have a friend named Lou. Pretty nice guy. He sells a special public speaking training course that works. You take the course, your fear will go away, and you will actually enjoy public speaking. Here is Lou's phone number. Give him a call. And, when I have my weekly meeting with Lou, I will give him your telephone number just in case you were not able to get in contact with him. He will solve your problem."

Done.

Because she trusted me, she never shopped for public speaking courses, or delayed. She simply called Lou right away. And when I gave Lou the pre-sold prospect the following week, he reported that she had already enrolled and her first class was later that week.

And three months later, she thanked me for the recommendation and said it was the best thing she had ever done for herself.

Pre-sold prospects are awesome to receive, and to give. Plus, the prospect benefits also by being introduced to a trusted source.

Type #2: The general information prospect.

Life isn't perfect and sometimes we don't have a strong personal relationship with prospects or clients. However, these prospects could still be great for your personal networking group members. Most members appreciate any type of prospect or lead. Let me give you an example.

At a school event with your children, you meet a person who is organizing a festival for next year. You don't have a personal relationship with this person, but you know that you have members that could get extra business if they just knew about the newly-planned festival, and who to contact.

Your insurance agent, your newspaper advertising salesman, your construction contractor, your professional clown, and your caterer would all like to have a chance to do business with your contact.

By providing them with the details of the person organizing the planned festival, they have a head start on their competition, and a fresh prospect for their business.

Not a perfect scenario, but a lot better than no leads or prospects at all.

Type #3: Anonymous prospects.

In this case, you know someone who needs the products or services of your members, but you can't use your name. This is the weakest type of lead, but it is still a lead.

For example, you are on the community board, and it would be a conflict of interest for you to recommend someone for an upcoming project. The project still needs products and services, but you can't use your name. At least your members know that they can bid on the project, even though you will not influence the decision.

Or, maybe your neighbor hates you, but yesterday a windstorm damaged his roof. He will still need a roofing contractor, but using your name might be detrimental.

The roofing contractor is happy to get the lead of someone who definitely needs a new roof.

Or if your group has a wedding planner, you might suggest contacting your ex-girlfriend who is getting married, but not use your name.

Any prospect or lead is appreciated.

Your goal is to make sure lots of prospects and leads are passed on regularly. This will hold the personal networking group together.

And the best strategy to get more prospects and leads?

Well, getting new members to join helps, but new members are untrained and haven't mastered how to pre-sell their current clients, and they also don't know much about their fellow members' businesses yet.

The best strategy is to highly train your current members to be masters at pre-selling their contacts. It is not unusual for a good member to bring five or six pre-sold prospects to a weekly meeting. Once the basic skill of pre-selling contacts is mastered, it is easy.

So concentrate on training your current members to do a better job of pre-selling to get the fastest results. But, also keep looking for new members too.

The social effect.

Small business owners and salespeople lead lonely lives. Their work consumes their lives. This means limited social contacts, and limited social time.

Your personal networking group could be the highlight of their week!

You will notice that some members will volunteer for any activity to help the group. Other members arrive 30 minutes early just to talk with their new, positive friends before your meeting starts.

Don't underestimate the social value that you provide to your members.

But also, don't let your club turn into a social visit instead of a group that works hard to provide each other with pre-sold prospects. Always remember the purpose of your group.

Your personal networking group also feeds your ego. You will feel important, because you are providing service to others, and it always feels good to be appreciated.

Your members will always remember you at Christmas, so I tell them in advance, "Dark chocolate is my favorite." ☺

And because your members do have relationships and social lives outside of your personal networking group, make sure to suspend your weekly meetings on holidays. Even the most dedicated business person needs a break.

Saying "thanks" for a great pre-sold prospect.

One of the fun social aspects is buying the meal for a fellow member. If you were the building contractor in the group, and the plumber gave you a pre-sold prospect that netted you $10,000 in commissions, you would of course love to buy the plumber his meal at the next weekly meeting.

Now, think of the possibilities of this simple "thank you" gesture of buying the member's meal.

Wouldn't you love to purchase the meal of six other members? Or wouldn't you love to have five people arguing over who could buy your meal? Sounds like too much fun.

Attendance and rules.

You will have to define how strict or how lenient you will be with the basic rules of your personal networking group. Here are some general problems you will have to address.

Attendance.

If the representative of a business category doesn't come, that means you are depriving another person the opportunity to be at your personal networking group. So how many absences will you tolerate?

Consider this. A person could be sick. Or on vacation. Or have a business problem that requires immediate attention. Or has to be out of town with clients.

Or, perhaps that person just doesn't care.

You will have to make a judgment on each individual case. Maybe you could say this, "If you can't come, please text in advance. And if you can't come for two consecutive meetings, please call. If you can't come for three consecutive meetings, please let another business person take your place."

Harsh? Well, let them know there are exceptions, and that is just a general guideline.

When someone does not come to your personal networking group, three bad things happen.

1. That person is not there to give the other members pre-sold prospects and leads.

2. When the other members bring pre-sold prospects and leads for that missing member, what do they do? Does that mean they have to go back to their client and apologize that they couldn't help them with a trusted referral?

3. The other members see the empty chair, and they start thinking, "Maybe I can just miss a few meetings whenever I want."

Bad members.

Bad members happen. Sometimes they are disrespectful, interrupt the meeting, heckle, complain and generally everyone hates them.

You will have to tactfully contact them after the meeting to let them know that the personal networking group is a private group, and as such, if they want to attend, they will have to abide by the courtesy rules the group has agreed upon. Usually that person never shows up again.

Takers? The people who never bring a single lead or pre-sold prospect, yet accept all the leads and pre-sold prospects others give to them?

Offer to have a private training with them. Teach them exactly what to say to their clients and contacts they meet every day. Remind them that to be a member of the group, they have to bring pre-sold prospects and leads for other members.

After several more weeks of no pre-sold prospects and leads from that member, tactfully let them know that this personal networking group isn't for them as they cannot meet the requirement of bringing new business to the other members.

Some members are professional complainers or have a welfare mentality. They want to receive pre-sold prospects immediately and will whine that the group isn't working for them.

It takes time for the other members to trust a new member, and time to understand their business. Results won't happen the first few weeks for most new members.

So if you have one or more of these impatient members, quietly agree with them that your personal networking group is a waste of their time, and purge that negativity from your group.

Door prize.

Yes, your rules can be positive also. After your group grows to 15 or 20 members, start a weekly door prize. Everyone loves a little bit of gambling for the entertainment value.

What can you provide for a weekly door prize?

Well, before you panic, your personal networking group will probably have a few people that are so in love with the group, they will volunteer to be in charge of this. You have to love volunteers.

Here are some door prize ideas:

1. Something donated by another member.

2. Something donated by the restaurant. A two-for-one dinner certificate or free pie. Mysteriously, I always won the free pie drawing. Must be karma.

3. A couple of lottery tickets for that week's super draw.

4. Certificates or samples from other businesses.

5. A few lessons for dance, karate, or cooking.

6. A free classified ad in the local paper or on the community website.

7. A free service call from a tradesman.

8. A gift certificate from a different restaurant.

Remember, the door prize is great advertising for someone, so finding door prizes is easy. Your members will quickly volunteer their services and products just for the advertising.

Dues.

Dues? Why? Everyone can buy his or her own breakfast. And most times when I went to the cashier to pay for my meal, the cashier said that the manager had "taken care of it" already. Yes, some restaurants really appreciate that you bring them more business.

Your personal networking group is all about getting new business, and not about running a club for profit. Of course you can charge dues, but then you are beginning to run another business, and you probably have enough on your hands with your current business.

Plus, one good referral would be more valuable than months and months of collected dues.

And what is your expense to run your personal networking group? The cost of your meal, and a little bit of your time. That's it. Even your meeting room is free since the restaurant has to seat you somewhere to eat.

By keeping the personal networking group as a service, and not a business, you only have to keep track of a membership list, and set up an email list or texting list to contact the members. You don't want a board of directors or minutes of your meetings. Keep it simple.

Speaking of a membership list, you can print out a list of the members, what they do, their contact information, and then give copies to everyone in the group. They can carry these copies with them, or even give copies to other people they know. Members will appreciate having this information at their fingertips.

What a great way to expand your reach of pre-sold prospects and leads for your business.

If your members insist on donating a few dollars, tell them to invest that money in tipping the waiter or waitress to make sure the group gets first-class service every time you meet.

Step #5: Duplicate.

As your personal networking group grows, more and more business people will be asking to join. Soon you will have 20 and maybe even up to 30 people in your group. When people see how well your members are prospering, they will want to be part of your group.

At 30 members, the personal networking group could lose its personal touch and might get a bit large to manage. Plus, you may have limited locations that can handle a group of 30+ people for your weekly meetings.

Now, you can decide to create a new personal networking group on a different day of the week in the same city, or even in another city. And if your business has employees or partners, you can get them to run the additional personal networking groups.

I find that the easiest way to duplicate is this:

1. Find a member in your current personal networking group who is excited about your group, responsible, and would love the chance to take over your personal networking group. Or, maybe replace yourself with a business associate who has been your assistant in organizing and running your personal networking group.

2. Then start a brand-new personal networking group. You should already have many new members waiting because their business category was already filled by your previous personal networking group. You will always have insurance agents, real estate agents, advertising salesmen and others waiting for a chance to belong to your group.

Plus, with your previous experience, you will find it easy to fill your new personal networking group.

Your second personal networking group.

This is easy. When you built your first personal networking group, many business categories filled quickly. You have a list of people who wanted to join, but there was already a member in that type of business.

Start with your waiting list. You may already have people waiting in these business categories:

- Life insurance

- Casualty insurance

- Roofing contractor

- Handyman

- Weight loss

- Health and vitamins

- Chiropractor

- Lawn and landscaping

- Car detailing

- Small business bookkeeping

- Lawyer

- Carpet cleaner

- Heating and air conditioning

- Small business consultant

- Car salesman

These members on your waiting list will want to join quickly because they will have the exclusive on that business category in your personal networking group. They are tired of being just one of a dozen other agents soliciting business at a Chamber of Commerce business card exchange.

You can be picky.

Because of your experience, you now are able to choose higher-quality members. And if you have any leftover drama or baggage with your original personal networking group, well, that can be left in the past. This is your chance to start new!

And you don't have a time restriction. Because you will already have a core base of members that want to join, you can take your time to get higher-quality members.

Why take a minimally-committed member who just wants to take leads from other members without creating reciprocal leads and pre-sold prospects? These types of takers are everywhere. You don't have to settle for them.

Instead, take a bit of time to look for quality members that will contribute quality leads and pre-sold prospects to your personal networking group.

Same restaurant?

Why not? You can have your second personal networking group meet at the same restaurant on a different day. You will be a VIP whenever you walk into that restaurant. They will love you.

But you could also have your new personal networking group at a different time of day, at a different location, or even a different city. You are in charge, and it is your group.

Be creative.

Most weekly personal networking groups meet for breakfast before most business is transacted during the business day. But don't limit your thinking just to breakfast.

I told you about the personal networking group in Montana that met for lunch at a Mexican restaurant every week.

Since I am more of an evening person, I love meeting once a week over dinner.

This book is only a guideline, so use your imagination!

You will grow as a leader.

Your personal networking group will look at you as not only a super connector and mentor, but also as a leader. You will grow from the experience of helping your personal networking group succeed.

Here are just a few things your group will ask you. And as you answer their questions and challenges, you will grow in expertise and experience.

- Will you please help me with my 30-second description of my business? I need it to be clearer so even my current customers will understand.

- What other marketing ideas do you have to help my business grow?

- Is there a good book you have read recently that you would recommend I get?

- Could you tell me what is wrong with this brochure? I pass it out, and no one calls me.

- How can I improve what I say so that the other members will send me more pre-sold prospects?

- I now know that I should make my contact details bigger on my business card. Should I leave my picture on my card?

- Where do you recommend that I look for some new, more dependable employees?

When we research and answer questions like these, we just naturally get better at what we do.

The research doesn't take much time. Some questions can be answered by Google. Others, by going to Amazon.com and getting a relevant book. For example, simple copywriting improvements could be learned quickly from my book, *How To Get Instant Trust, Belief, Influence And Rapport! 13 Ways To Create Open Minds By Talking To The Subconscious Mind.*

Sometimes just a single tip, such as sending out thank-you cards to your customers, is all it takes to move a member's business forward.

Maybe you could start each weekly meeting with a new marketing tip that everyone could use. How long would it take to find one? Less than ten minutes. Investing a little time helping your members always pays off ... for everyone.

Other networking groups.

Yes, there are other networking groups that your members can join. However, people follow leaders. Since you will be an effective leader of your personal networking group, your weekly meeting will become their priority.

Now, if your members add the Chamber of Commerce, BNI, or another networking group to their marketing, because of your training and help, they will be more effective in their additional groups. They won't be a member that simply pays dues, sits on the sidelines, and suffers with minimal results. They will be more proactive to make their time and money investments in those groups pay off.

Now it is up to you to change how you get your prospects.

* Forget cold-calling.

* Forget cold leads.

* Forget expensive advertising.

* Forget lukewarm referrals.

Embrace **pre-sold** prospects coming to you regularly by creating your own personal networking group.

And not only will you help your business, but you will also be providing a tremendous service to others.

FREE!

Get 7 mini-reports of amazing, easy sentences that create new, hot prospects.

Discover how just a few correct words can change your network marketing results forever.

Get all seven free Big Al mini-reports, and the free weekly Big Al Report with more recruiting and prospecting tips.

Sign up today at:

http://www.BigAlReport.com

MORE BIG AL RESOURCES

Want Big Al to speak in your area?

Request a Big Al training event:

http://www.BigAlSeminars.com

Books by Tom "Big Al" Schreiter are available at:

http://www.BigAlBooks.com

See a full line of Big Al products at:

http://www.FortuneNow.com

ABOUT THE AUTHOR

Tom "Big Al" Schreiter has 40+ years of experience in network marketing and MLM. As the author of the original "Big Al" training books in the late '70s, he has continued to speak in over 80 countries on using the exact words and phrases to get prospects to open up their minds and say "YES."

His passion is marketing ideas, marketing campaigns, and how to speak to the subconscious mind in simplified, practical ways. He is always looking for case studies of incredible marketing campaigns that give usable lessons.

As the author of numerous audio trainings, Tom is a favorite speaker at company conventions and regional events.

His blog, **http://www.BigAlBlog.com** is a regular update of network marketing and MLM business-building ideas.

Anyone can subscribe to his free weekly tips at:

http://www.BigAlReport.com

11873775R00054

Printed in Great Britain
by Amazon.co.uk, Ltd.,
Marston Gate.